# REH ★ PROLESSONS

## JAZZ-ROCK LICKS for Guitar

CD INCLUDED

by
**Steve Freeman**

ISBN 978-1-4234-9457-7

HAL•LEONARD®
CORPORATION

7777 W. BLUEMOUND RD. P.O. BOX 13819 MILWAUKEE, WI 53213

In Australia Contact:
**Hal Leonard Australia Pty. Ltd.**
4 Lentara Court
Cheltenham, Victoria, 3192 Australia
Email: ausadmin@halleonard.com.au

Visit Hal Leonard Online at
**www.halleonard.com**

# Table of Contents

# Introduction

The philosophy of the REH Pro Licks series is to give you a larger and varied vocabulary of licks and melodic ideas. Many guitarists strive to have their own original style and therefore feel they shouldn't copy licks from other players. In reality, it's very beneficial, if not necessary, to study the ideas of other players. The benefits of doing so are numerous:

- **Developing the ear** – By playing and singing these lines, you'll begin to hear and understand melodies and how they relate to chords.
- **Building technique and confidence** – These Pro Licks are great for building chops and will provide you with a large arsenal on which to rely.
- **Music theory** – As these lines are all constructed from various scales, arpeggios, and intervals, important insights into music theory can be gained by studying them.

Once you learn these lines, or the lines of any other players you study, you'll find innumerable ways to alter them and "make them your own." This process of assimilation and manipulation is key in developing your own style.

Here are some additional suggestions to help you get the most out of the Pro Licks:

- Play them in all keys and, if possible, in different octaves.
- Since many of the lines are written in simple sixteenth notes for quick learning, experiment by using different rhythms or by starting them in different parts of the measure, etc.
- Feel free to experiment with different articulations by employing hammer-ons, pull-offs, slides, bends, etc.
- Try the licks out over other chords than the ones suggested.
- Make adjustments to the suggested fingerings, if necessary, to make the lines more playable and comfortable.
- Try to work these lines, in whole or in part, into your playing as soon as possible.

Each Pro Lick has a few suggested chords over which it can be played. These are usually basic seventh chords (i.e., A7, Bm7, Cmaj7, etc.). The following list shows extension and substitution possibilities (using the C root as an example) over which the lines will also work:

C7 = C9, C11, C7sus4, C13, B♭/C, C7/B♭
Cm7 = Cm9, Cm11, C7sus4, Cm6, E♭/C
Cmaj7 = C6, Cmaj9, Cmaj13, C6/9, G/C

 **Intro to CD**

**Editor's note:** Each Pro Lick is demonstrated on the CD twice on separate tracks—once at full speed with a full band, and once slowly by itself. Also, note that the basic lick has been notated in the book, but some tracks feature additional improvisatory phrases tacked on to the end. Once you learn the notated lick, try to figure out the improvised portion at the end.

 Pro Lick #1

The first measure of this line is constructed with four-note arpeggios diatonic to the key of E♭ major (beat 1 = A♭maj7, beat 2 = Dm7♭5, beat 3 = E♭). Notice the use of chromaticism, which helps to connect the positions smoothly.

Will also work over: Fm7

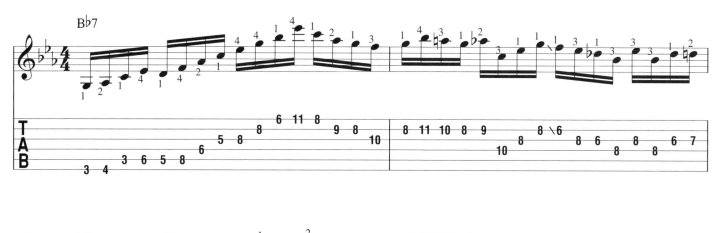

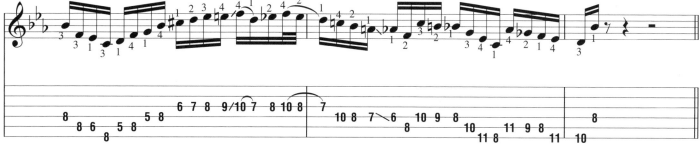

 Pro Lick #2

This phrase is constructed from the B melodic minor scale (B–C♯–D–E–F♯–G♯–A♯) or E Lydian dominant. The A♯ (or B♭) note, which is the ♭5th of E, is featured prominently throughout. Try using hammer-ons and pull-offs in this phrase in addition to alternate picking.

Will also work over: Bm7 and E7

 **Pro Lick #3**

This is a continuation of the previous line. Connecting ideas and phrases together really aids in understanding the fretboard. It also helps build technique and gives you a larger vocabulary of ideas.

Will also work over: Bm7 and E7

 **Pro Lick #4**

This line utilizes the C minor (or E♭ major) pentatonic scale. Since the major pentatonic scale contains no 7th, it can also be used over major and dominant chords.

Will also work over: E♭maj7

# Pro Lick #5

This is a modern-sounding line utilizing 4th interval shapes. The use of alternate picking is required to sound smooth and even. Notice that the entire line is played in seventh position.

Will also work over: Am7

# Pro Lick #6

This line is primarily made up of 4ths and arpeggios. Notice that beat 4 of measure 1 and beat 1 of measure 2 outline Bm7 and Amaj7, respectively.

Will also work over: Em7

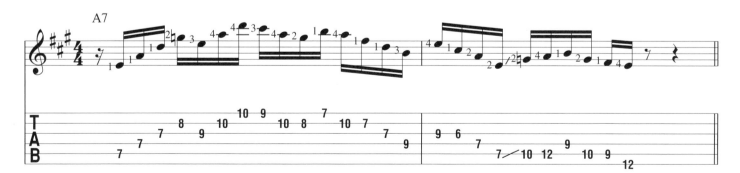

## ◆14 ◆15 Pro Lick #7

Chromaticism plays a big role in this line. Pay attention to the given fingering, as it will help connect the positions smoothly. Notice the G and A triads in measures 7 and 8.

Will also work over: A7

## ◆16 ◆17 Pro Lick #8

The phrasing is the most important aspect of this lick. Pay close attention to the slides and L.H. fingerings.

## ◆18 ◆19 Pro Lick #9

This lick is more at home in a blues or bebop context. Be sure to notice the hammer/pull move used on the "a" of beat 2 of the first measure. This is essential to making the lick sound smooth.

## ◆20 ◆21 Pro Lick #10

Here's a nice ii–V–I lick in C. Over the ii chord (Dm7), we use an Fmaj7 arpeggio, which is its diatonic substitute. Over the G7 chord, we use an F melodic minor scale (F–G–A♭–B♭–C–D–E) to create an altered sound (G7♭9/♯9).

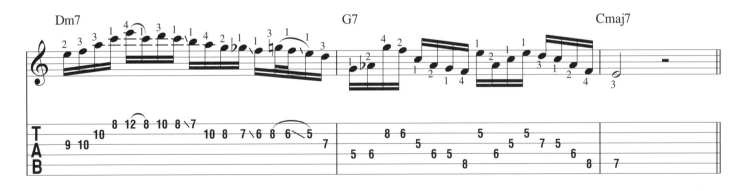

## Pro Lick #11

Here's another one that's more on the blues/jazz side. Experiment with different fingerings to keep it in one position.

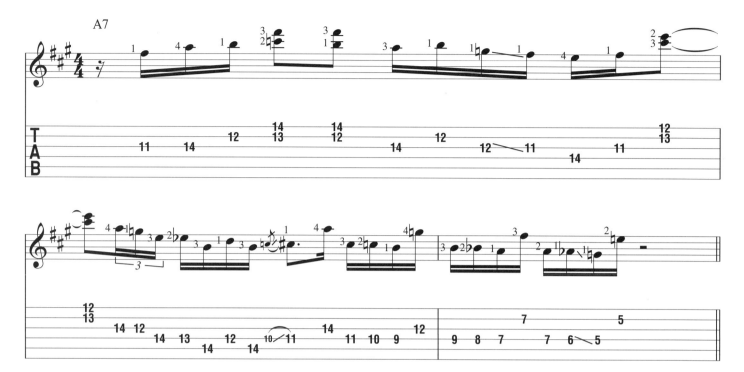

## Pro Lick #12

This is an etude built from the C harmonic minor scale (C–D–E♭–F–G–A♭–B). It works through all five fingering patterns using triads (G and A♭) and four-note arpeggios diatonic to the scale. Break this line apart and learn it in four-measure sections.

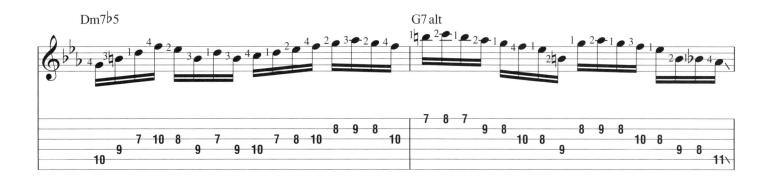

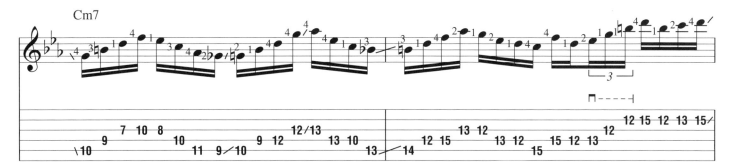

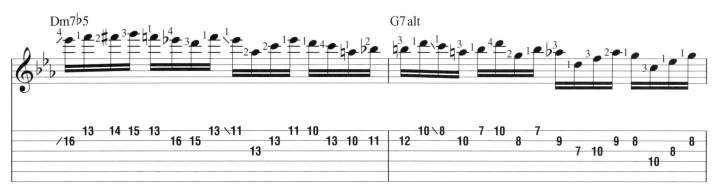

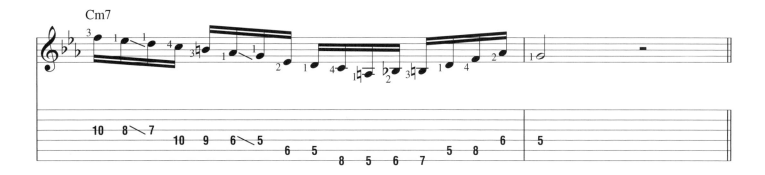

## Pro Lick #13

Chromatics, octaves, and 6ths dominate this phrase. Try employing both legato and alternate picking approaches. The fingering is essential for making the line flow smoothly.

Will also work over: D7

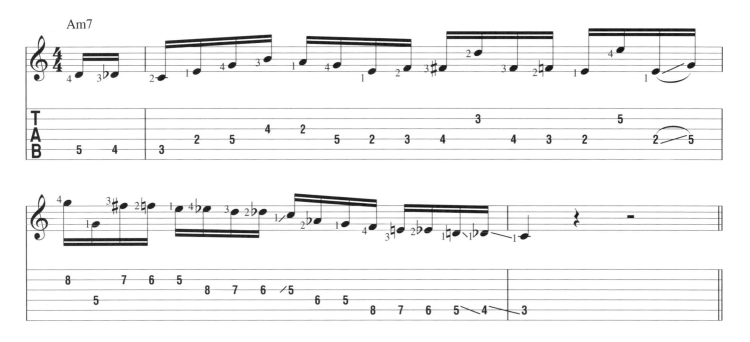

## Pro Lick #14

Here's a chromatic idea that's great for connecting positions. It begins in tenth position and winds down to fifth by the end.

Will also work over: F7

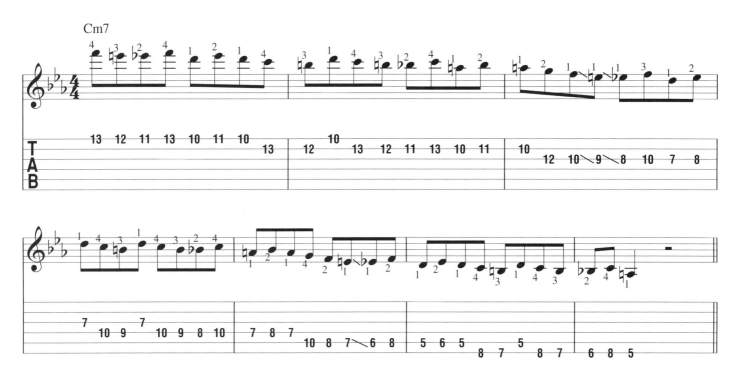

# ◆30◆ ◆31◆ Pro Lick #15

This line hints at the B melodic minor scale (B–C♯–D–E–F♯–G♯–A♯), also known as the E Lydian dominant scale. It also uses a lot of chromatic passing tones and arpeggios diatonic to the key of A major.

Will also work over: Bm7

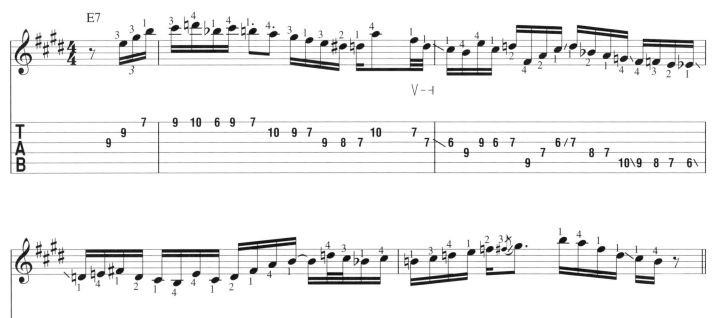

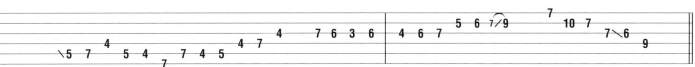

# ◆32◆ ◆33◆ Pro Lick #16

This is a traditional bebop phrase that also works well over a ii–V–i in A minor (Bm7♭5–E7♯9–Am7). Chromatic approach notes are employed through much of measures 1 and 2, while measures 3 and 4 draw from A melodic minor (A–B–C–D–E–F♯–G♯).

Will also work over: D7

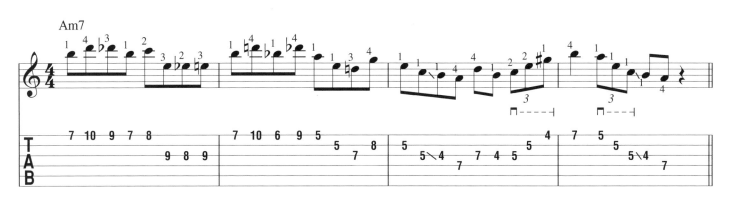

This line is built from four-note arpeggios diatonic to B♭ major. In measure 1, Gm7 and E♭maj7 arpeggios are used; in measure 2, we use E♭maj7, Dm7, Cm7, and B♭maj7. The final measure contains a chromatic line that resolves to C, the 5th of F7.

Will also work over: Cm7

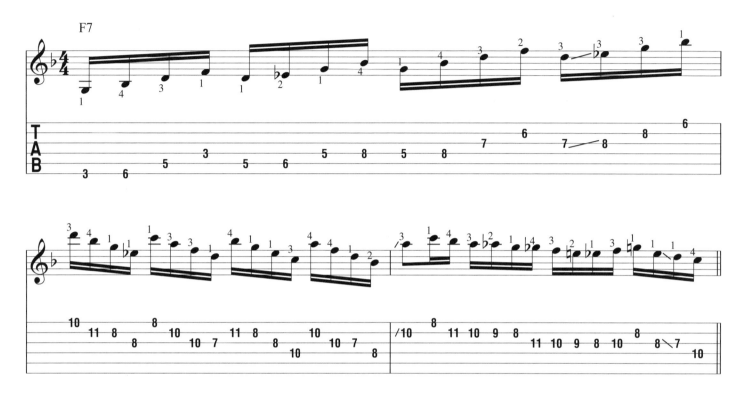

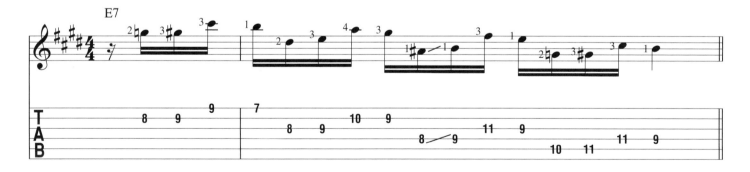

**36** **37** Pro Lick #18

This is a short line using *chromatic approach notes*—i.e., notes that approach chord tones from a half step above or below.

Will also work over: E♭maj7

 **Pro Lick #19**

This line sounds nice played with legato techniques. Notice the chromaticism and four-note arpeggios throughout (Dm9 and Am7).

Will also work over: G7

 **Pro Lick #20**

This phrase can be used over a static Cm7 chord or a ii–V–i progression in C minor (Dm7♭5–G7alt–Cm7). Here, we're mixing the *C harmonic minor scale* (C–D–E♭–F–G–A♭–B) and the *C blues scale* (C–E♭–F–F♯–G–B♭).

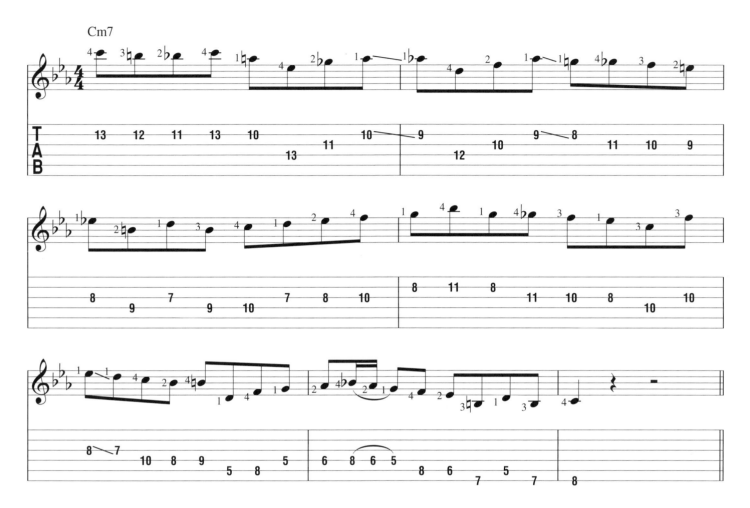

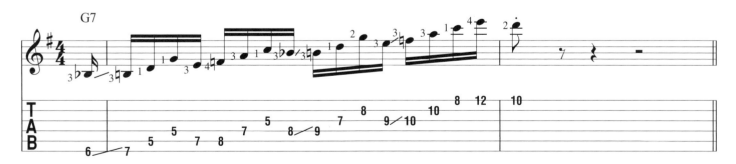

**Pro Lick #21**

This lick is built from using two major triads a whole step apart: G and F. Notice the chromatic approach note that leads into each triad.

Will also work over: Dm7

16

# Pro Lick #22

This etude is a combination of many short melodic phrases. It should be taken apart and learned in sections. See how many ideas from the rest of the book you can find in this one.

Will also work over: Bm7

## 46 47 Pro Lick #23

This line works over a ii–V–I in B♭ major (Cm7–F7–B♭maj7). Be sure to pay attention to the phrasing and slides in this one.

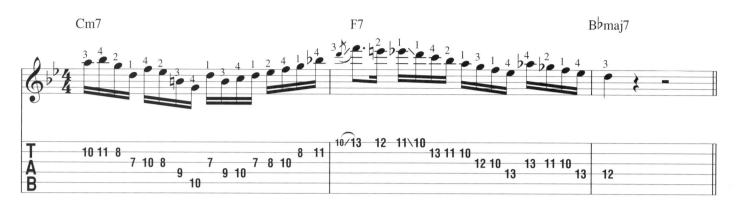

## 48 49 Pro Lick #24

This etude is a combination of diminished and melodic minor ideas. Notice the triad shapes (F and B) in the first line. Much of the rest of the line contains four-note arpeggios from C melodic minor (or F Lydian dominant): C–D–E♭–F–G–A–B.

Will also work over: Cm7

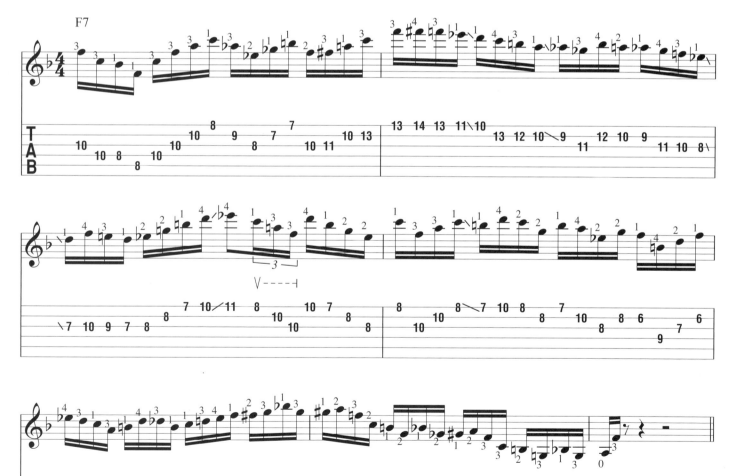

# About the Author

A part of the music business for 25 years, Steve Freeman studied at Berklee College of Music in Boston, MA and Musicians Institute (MI) in Hollywood, CA. After his graduation, he joined the MI staff and taught there for six years. At MI, Steve had the opportunity to play and teach with such artists as Don Mock, Scott Henderson, Steve Trovato, Tommy Tedesco, Joe Diorio, Jeff Berlin, and Robben Ford, to name a few. While in California, Steve was also an active studio session guitarist for Japanese radio and television.

In 1985, Steve founded the Atlanta Institute of Music—a nationally accredited music school for guitar, bass, and drums—where he acts as President and serves on the faculty as well. In Atlanta, Steve has performed and/ or recorded with Oteil and Kofi Burbrige, Jeff Sipe, Dr. Dan Matrazzo, Randy Hoexter, Geof McBride, and the Guild of Sound.

Steve has authored three books: *Jazz Rock* and *Jazz Pro Lick Series* (REH/Hal Leonard Publications) and *Fusion Guitar* (Warner Brothers Publications).

Steve currently resides in Atlanta and is the National Director for Camp Jam (*www.campjam.com*). Steve actively composes, records, and teaches in the Atlanta area and is releasing a new CD entitled *Surfside* in 2010. Visit Steve online at *www.stevefreemanguitarist.com*.

 Closing

# GUITAR NOTATION LEGEND

Guitar music can be notated three different ways: on a *musical staff*, in *tablature*, and in *rhythm slashes*.

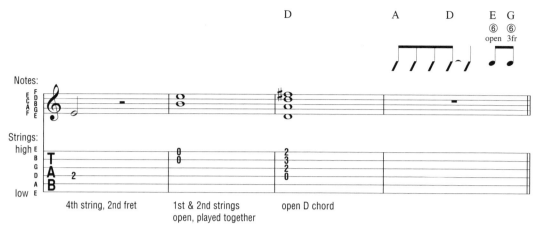

**RHYTHM SLASHES** are written above the staff. Strum chords in the rhythm indicated. Use the chord diagrams found at the top of the first page of the transcription for the appropriate chord voicings. Round noteheads indicate single notes.

**THE MUSICAL STAFF** shows pitches and rhythms and is divided by bar lines into measures. Pitches are named after the first seven letters of the alphabet.

**TABLATURE** graphically represents the guitar fingerboard. Each horizontal line represents a string, and each number represents a fret.

4th string, 2nd fret | 1st & 2nd strings open, played together | open D chord

# Definitions for Special Guitar Notation

**HALF-STEP BEND:** Strike the note and bend up 1/2 step.

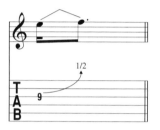

**WHOLE-STEP BEND:** Strike the note and bend up one step.

**GRACE NOTE BEND:** Strike the note and immediately bend up as indicated.

**SLIGHT (MICROTONE) BEND:** Strike the note and bend up 1/4 step.

**BEND AND RELEASE:** Strike the note and bend up as indicated, then release back to the original note. Only the first note is struck.

**PRE-BEND:** Bend the note as indicated, then strike it.

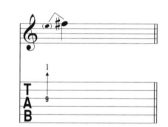

**PRE-BEND AND RELEASE:** Bend the note as indicated. Strike it and release the bend back to the original note.

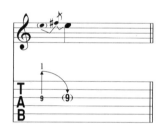

**UNISON BEND:** Strike the two notes simultaneously and bend the lower note up to the pitch of the higher.

**VIBRATO:** The string is vibrated by rapidly bending and releasing the note with the fretting hand.

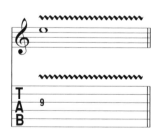

**WIDE VIBRATO:** The pitch is varied to a greater degree by vibrating with the fretting hand.

**HAMMER-ON:** Strike the first (lower) note with one finger, then sound the higher note (on the same string) with another finger by fretting it without picking.

**PULL-OFF:** Place both fingers on the notes to be sounded. Strike the first note and without picking, pull the finger off to sound the second (lower) note.

**LEGATO SLIDE:** Strike the first note and then slide the same fret-hand finger up or down to the second note. The second note is not struck.

**SHIFT SLIDE:** Same as legato slide, except the second note is struck.

**TRILL:** Very rapidly alternate between the notes indicated by continuously hammering on and pulling off.

**TAPPING:** Hammer ("tap") the fret indicated with the pick-hand index or middle finger and pull off to the note fretted by the fret hand.

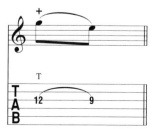

**NATURAL HARMONIC:** Strike the note while the fret-hand lightly touches the string directly over the fret indicated.

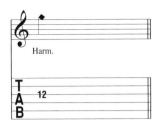

**PINCH HARMONIC:** The note is fretted normally and a harmonic is produced by adding the edge of the thumb or the tip of the index finger of the pick hand to the normal pick attack.

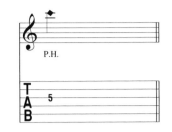

**HARP HARMONIC:** The note is fretted normally and a harmonic is produced by gently resting the pick hand's index finger directly above the indicated fret (in parentheses) while the pick hand's thumb or pick assists by plucking the appropriate string.

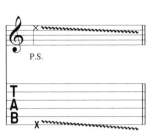

**PICK SCRAPE:** The edge of the pick is rubbed down (or up) the string, producing a scratchy sound.

**MUFFLED STRINGS:** A percussive sound is produced by laying the fret hand across the string(s) without depressing, and striking them with the pick hand.

**PALM MUTING:** The note is partially muted by the pick hand lightly touching the string(s) just before the bridge.

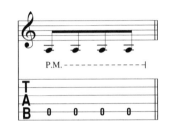

**RAKE:** Drag the pick across the strings indicated with a single motion.

**TREMOLO PICKING:** The note is picked as rapidly and continuously as possible.

**ARPEGGIATE:** Play the notes of the chord indicated by quickly rolling them from bottom to top.

**VIBRATO BAR DIVE AND RETURN:** The pitch of the note or chord is dropped a specified number of steps (in rhythm), then returned to the original pitch.

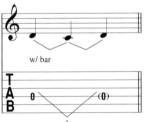

**VIBRATO BAR SCOOP:** Depress the bar just before striking the note, then quickly release the bar.

**VIBRATO BAR DIP:** Strike the note and then immediately drop a specified number of steps, then release back to the original pitch.

# Additional Musical Definitions

| | | |
|---|---|---|
| (accent) | • Accentuate note (play it louder). | |
| (accent) | • Accentuate note with great intensity. | |
| (staccato) | • Play the note short. | |
| ⊓ | • Downstroke | |
| V | • Upstroke | |

| | |
|---|---|
| **D.S. al Coda** | • Go back to the sign (𝄋), then play until the measure marked "*To Coda*," then skip to the section labelled "**Coda**." |
| **D.C. al Fine** | • Go back to the beginning of the song and play until the measure marked "*Fine*" (end). |

| | |
|---|---|
| **Rhy. Fig.** | • Label used to recall a recurring accompaniment pattern (usually chordal). |
| **Riff** | • Label used to recall composed, melodic lines (usually single notes) which recur. |
| **Fill** | • Label used to identify a brief melodic figure which is to be inserted into the arrangement. |
| **Rhy. Fill** | • A chordal version of a Fill. |
| tacet | • Instrument is silent (drops out). |
| | • Repeat measures between signs. |
| | • When a repeated section has different endings, play the first ending only the first time and the second ending only the second time. |

**NOTE:** Tablature numbers in parentheses mean:
1. The note is being sustained over a system (note in standard notation is tied), or
2. The note is sustained, but a new articulation (such as a hammer-on, pull-off, slide or vibrato) begins, or
3. The note is a barely audible "ghost" note (note in standard notation is also in parentheses).

# GUITAR *signature licks*

Signature Licks book/CD packs provide a step-by-step breakdown of "right from the record" riffs, licks, and solos so you can jam along with your favorite bands. They contain performance notes and an overview of each artist's or group's style, with note-for-note transcriptions in notes and tab. The CDs feature full-band demos at both normal and slow speeds.

**ACOUSTIC CLASSICS**
00695864 .....................$19.95

**AEROSMITH 1973-1979**
00695106 .....................$22.95

**AEROSMITH 1979-1998**
00695219 .....................$22.95

**BEST OF AGGRO-METAL**
00695592 .....................$19.95

**DUANE ALLMAN**
00696042 .....................$22.95

**BEST OF CHET ATKINS**
00695752 .....................$22.95

**THE BEACH BOYS DEFINITIVE COLLECTION**
00695683 .....................$22.95

**BEST OF THE BEATLES FOR ACOUSTIC GUITAR**
00695453 .....................$22.95

**THE BEATLES BASS**
00695283 .....................$22.95

**THE BEATLES FAVORITES**
00695096 .....................$24.95

**THE BEATLES HITS**
00695049 .....................$24.95

**BEST OF GEORGE BENSON**
00695418 .....................$22.95

**BEST OF BLACK SABBATH**
00695249 .....................$22.95

**BEST OF BLINK - 182**
00695704 .....................$22.95

**BEST OF BLUES GUITAR**
00695846 .....................$19.95

**BLUES GUITAR CLASSICS**
00695177 .....................$19.95

**BLUES/ROCK GUITAR MASTERS**
00695348 .....................$21.95

**KENNY BURRELL**
00695830 .....................$22.99

**BEST OF CHARLIE CHRISTIAN**
00695584 .....................$22.95

**BEST OF ERIC CLAPTON**
00695038 .....................$24.95

**ERIC CLAPTON – THE BLUESMAN**
00695040 .....................$22.95

**ERIC CLAPTON – FROM THE ALBUM UNPLUGGED**
00695250 .....................$24.95

**BEST OF CREAM**
00695251 .....................$22.95

**CREEDANCE CLEARWATER REVIVAL**
00695924 .....................$22.95

**DEEP PURPLE – GREATEST HITS**
00695625 .....................$22.95

**THE BEST OF DEF LEPPARD**
00696516 .....................$22.95

**THE DOORS**
00695373 .....................$22.95

**ESSENTIAL JAZZ GUITAR**
00695875 .....................$19.99

**FAMOUS ROCK GUITAR SOLOS**
00695590 .....................$19.95

**BEST OF FOO FIGHTERS**
00695481 .....................$24.95

**ROBBEN FORD**
00695903 .....................$22.95

**GREATEST GUITAR SOLOS OF ALL TIME**
00695301 .....................$19.95

**BEST OF GRANT GREEN**
00695747 .....................$22.95

**BEST OF GUNS N' ROSES**
00695183 .....................$24.95

**THE BEST OF BUDDY GUY**
00695186 .....................$22.95

**JIM HALL**
00695848 .....................$22.99

**HARD ROCK SOLOS**
00695591 .....................$19.95

**JIMI HENDRIX**
00696560 .....................$24.95

**JIMI HENDRIX – VOLUME 2**
00695835 .....................$24.95

**JOHN LEE HOOKER**
00695894 .....................$19.99

**HOT COUNTRY GUITAR**
00695580 .....................$19.95

**BEST OF JAZZ GUITAR**
00695586 .....................$24.95

**ERIC JOHNSON**
00699317 .....................$24.95

**ROBERT JOHNSON**
00695264 .....................$22.95

**BARNEY KESSEL**
00696009 .....................$22.99

**THE ESSENTIAL ALBERT KING**
00695713 .....................$22.95

**B.B. KING – THE DEFINITIVE COLLECTION**
00695635 .....................$22.95

**B.B. KING – MASTER BLUESMAN**
00699923 .....................$24.99

**THE KINKS**
00695553 .....................$22.95

**BEST OF KISS**
00699413 .....................$22.95

**MARK KNOPFLER**
00695178 .....................$22.95

**LYNYRD SKYNYRD**
00695872 .....................$24.95

**BEST OF YNGWIE MALMSTEEN**
00695669 .....................$22.95

**BEST OF PAT MARTINO**
00695632 .....................$24.99

**WES MONTGOMERY**
00695387 .....................$24.95

**BEST OF NIRVANA**
00695483 .....................$24.95

**THE OFFSPRING**
00695852 .....................$24.95

**VERY BEST OF OZZY OSBOURNE**
00695431 .....................$22.95

**BEST OF JOE PASS**
00695730 .....................$22.95

**TOM PETTY**
00696021 .....................$22.99

**PINK FLOYD – EARLY CLASSICS**
00695566 .....................$22.95

**THE POLICE**
00695724 .....................$22.95

**THE GUITARS OF ELVIS**
00696507 .....................$22.95

**BEST OF QUEEN**
00695097 .....................$24.95

**BEST OF RAGE AGAINST THE MACHINE**
00695480 .....................$24.95

**RED HOT CHILI PEPPERS**
00695173 .....................$22.95

**RED HOT CHILI PEPPERS – GREATEST HITS**
00695828 .....................$24.95

**BEST OF DJANGO REINHARDT**
00695660 .....................$24.95

**BEST OF ROCK**
00695884 .....................$19.95

**BEST OF ROCK 'N' ROLL GUITAR**
00695559 .....................$19.95

**BEST OF ROCKABILLY GUITAR**
00695785 .....................$19.95

**THE ROLLING STONES**
00695079 .....................$24.95

**BEST OF DAVID LEE ROTH**
00695843 .....................$24.95

**BEST OF JOE SATRIANI**
00695216 .....................$22.95

**BEST OF SILVERCHAIR**
00695488 .....................$22.95

**THE BEST OF SOUL GUITAR**
00695703 .....................$19.95

**BEST OF SOUTHERN ROCK**
00695560 .....................$19.95

**MIKE STERN**
00695800 .....................$24.99

**ROD STEWART**
00695663 .....................$22.95

**BEST OF SURF GUITAR**
00695822 .....................$19.95

**BEST OF SYSTEM OF A DOWN**
00695788 .....................$22.95

**ROCK BAND**
00696063 .....................$22.99

**ROBIN TROWER**
00695950 .....................$22.95

**STEVE VAI**
00673247 .....................$22.95

**STEVE VAI – ALIEN LOVE SECRETS: THE NAKED VAMPS**
00695223 .....................$22.95

**STEVE VAI – FIRE GARDEN: THE NAKED VAMPS**
00695166 .....................$22.95

**STEVE VAI – THE ULTRA ZONE: NAKED VAMPS**
00695684 .....................$22.95

**STEVIE RAY VAUGHAN – 2ND ED.**
00699316 .....................$24.95

**THE GUITAR STYLE OF STEVIE RAY VAUGHAN**
00695155 .....................$24.95

**BEST OF THE VENTURES**
00695772 .....................$19.95

**THE WHO – 2ND ED.**
00695561 .....................$22.95

**JOHNNY WINTER**
00695951 .....................$22.99

**BEST OF ZZ TOP**
00695738 .....................$24.95

FOR MORE INFORMATION,
SEE YOUR LOCAL MUSIC DEALER,
OR WRITE TO:

HAL•LEONARD® CORPORATION
7777 W. BLUEMOUND RD. P.O. BOX 13819
MILWAUKEE, WISCONSIN 53213

**www.halleonard.com**

**COMPLETE DESCRIPTIONS AND SONGLISTS ONLINE!**
Prices, contents and availability subject to change without notice.

0410

# PLAY THE CLASSICS
## JAZZ FOLIOS FOR GUITARISTS

### BEST OF JAZZ GUITAR
*by Wolf Marshall • Signature Licks*

**INCLUDES TAB**

In this book/CD pack, Wolf Marshall provides a hands-on analysis of 10 of the most frequently played tunes in the jazz genre, as played by the leading guitarists of all time. Features: All the Things You Are • How Insensitive • I'll Remember April • So What • Yesterdays • and more.
00695586 Book/CD Pack......................................$24.95

### GUITAR STANDARDS
*Classic Jazz Masters Series*

**INCLUDES TAB**

16 classic jazz guitar performances transcribed note for note with tablature: All of You (Kenny Burrell) • Easter Parade (Herb Ellis) • I'll Remember April (Grant Green) • Lover Man (Django Reinhardt) • Song for My Father (George Benson) • The Way You Look Tonight (Wes Montgomery) • and more. Includes a discography.
00699143 Guitar Transcriptions ..........................$14.95

### JAZZ CLASSICS
*Jazz Guitar Chord Melody Solos*
*arr. Jeff Arnold*

**INCLUDES TAB**

27 rich arrangements of jazz classics: Blue in Green • Bluesette • Doxy • Epistrophy • Footprints • Giant Steps • Lush Life • A Night in Tunisia • Nuages • St. Thomas • Waltz for Debby • Yardbird Suite • and more.
00699758 Solo Guitar .........................................$12.95

### JAZZ CLASSICS FOR SOLO GUITAR
*arranged by Robert B. Yelin*

**INCLUDES TAB**

This collection includes excellent chord melody arrangements in standard notation and tablature for 35 all-time jazz favorites: April in Paris • Cry Me a River • Day by Day • God Bless' the Child • It Might as Well Be Spring • Lover • My Romance • Nuages • Satin Doll • Tenderly • Unchained Melody • Wave • and more!
00699279 Solo Guitar .........................................$17.95

### JAZZ FAVORITES FOR SOLO GUITAR
*arranged by Robert B. Yelin*

**INCLUDES TAB**

This fantastic 35-song collection includes lush chord melody arrangements in standard notation and tab: Autumn in New York • Call Me Irresponsible • How Deep Is the Ocean • I Could Write a Book • The Lady Is a Tramp • Mood Indigo • Polka Dots and Moonbeams • Solitude • Take the "A" Train • Where or When • more.
00699278 Solo Guitar .........................................$17.95

### JAZZ FOR THE ROCK GUITARIST
*by Michael Mueller*

**INCLUDES TAB**

Take your playing beyond barre chords and the blues box! This book/CD pack will take you through the essentials of the jazz idiom with plenty of exercises and examples – all of which are demonstrated on the accompanying CD.
00695856 Book/CD Pack......................................$14.95

### JAZZ GEMS FOR SOLO GUITAR
*arranged by Robert B. Yelin*

**INCLUDES TAB**

35 great solo arrangements of jazz classics, including: After You've Gone • Alice in Wonderland • The Christmas Song • Four • Meditation • Stompin' at the Savoy • Sweet and Lovely • Waltz for Debby • Yardbird Suite • You'll Never Walk Alone • You've Changed • and more.
00699617 Solo Guitar .........................................$17.95

### JAZZ GUITAR BIBLE

**INCLUDES TAB**

The one book that has all of the jazz guitar classics transcribed note-for-note, with standard notation and tablature. Includes over 30 songs: Body and Soul • Girl Talk • I'll Remember April • In a Sentimental Mood • My Funny Valentine • Nuages • Satin Doll • So What • Stardust • Take Five • Tangerine • Yardbird Suite • and more.
00690466 Guitar Recorded Versions ....................$19.95

### JAZZ GUITAR CHORD MELODIES
*arranged & performed by Dan Towey*

**INCLUDES TAB**

This book/CD pack includes complete solo performances of 12 standards, including: All the Things You Are • Body and Soul • My Romance • How Insensitive • My One and Only Love • and more. The arrangements are performance level and range in difficulty from intermediate to advanced.
00698988 Book/CD Pack ...................................$19.95

### JAZZ GUITAR PLAY-ALONG
*Guitar Play-Along Volume 16*

**INCLUDES TAB**

With this book/CD pack, all you have to do is follow the tab, listen to the CD to hear how the guitar should sound, and then play along using the separate backing tracks. 8 songs: All Blues • Bluesette • Footprints • How Insensitive (Insensatez) • Misty • Satin Doll • Stella by Starlight • Tenor Madness.
00699584 Book/CD Pack ...................................$15.95

### JAZZ STANDARDS FOR FINGERSTYLE GUITAR

**INCLUDES TAB**

20 songs, including: All the Things You Are • Autumn Leaves • Bluesette • Body and Soul • Fly Me to the Moon • The Girl from Ipanema • How Insensitive • I've Grown Accustomed to Her Face • My Funny Valentine • Satin Doll • Stompin' at the Savoy • and more.
00699029 Fingerstyle Guitar ...............................$10.95

### JAZZ STANDARDS FOR SOLO GUITAR
*arranged by Robert B. Yelin*

**INCLUDES TAB**

35 chord melody guitar arrangements, including: Ain't Misbehavin' • Autumn Leaves • Bewitched • Cherokee • Darn That Dream • Girl Talk • I've Got You Under My Skin • Lullaby of Birdland • My Funny Valentine • A Nightingale Sang in Berkeley Square • Stella by Starlight • The Very Thought of You • and more.
00699277 Solo Guitar .........................................$17.95

### 101 MUST-KNOW JAZZ LICKS
*by Wolf Marshall*

**INCLUDES TAB**

Add a jazz feel and flavor to your playing! 101 definitive licks, plus a demonstration CD, from every major jazz guitar style, neatly organized into easy-to-use categories. They're all here: swing and pre-bop, bebop, post-bop modern jazz, hard bop and cool jazz, modal jazz, soul jazz and postmodern jazz.
00695433 Book/CD Pack......................................$17.95

FOR MORE INFORMATION, SEE YOUR LOCAL MUSIC DEALER, OR WRITE TO:

**HAL•LEONARD® CORPORATION**
7777 W. BLUEMOUND RD. P.O. BOX 13819 MILWAUKEE, WI 53213
Visit Hal Leonard Online at **www.halleonard.com**

*Prices, contents and availability subject to change without notice.*

0508

# Get Better at Guitar

## ...with these Great Guitar Instruction Books from Hal Leonard!

### 101 GUITAR TIPS
STUFF ALL THE PROS KNOW AND USE
*by Adam St. James*
This book contains invaluable guidance on everything from scales and music theory to truss rod adjustments, proper recording studio set-ups, and much more. The book also features snippets of advice from some of the most celebrated guitarists and producers in the music business, including B.B. King, Steve Vai, Joe Satriani, Warren Haynes, Laurence Juber, Pete Anderson, Tom Dowd and others, culled from the author's hundreds of interviews.
00695737 Book/CD Pack.........................$16.95

### AMAZING PHRASING
50 WAYS TO IMPROVE YOUR IMPROVISATIONAL SKILLS
*by Tom Kolb*
This book/CD pack explores all the main components necessary for crafting well-balanced rhythmic and melodic phrases. It also explains how these phrases are put together to form cohesive solos. Many styles are covered – rock, blues, jazz, fusion, country, Latin, funk and more – and all of the concepts are backed up with musical examples. The companion CD contains 89 demos for listening, and most tracks feature full-band backing.
00695583 Book/CD Pack.........................$19.95

### BLUES YOU CAN USE
*by John Ganapes*
A comprehensive source designed to help guitarists develop both lead and rhythm playing. Covers: Texas, Delta, R&B, early rock and roll, gospel, blues/rock and more. Includes: 21 complete solos • chord progressions and riffs • turnarounds • moveable scales and more. CD features leads and full band backing.
00695007 Book/CD Pack.........................$19.95

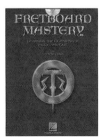

### FRETBOARD MASTERY
*by Troy Stetina*
Untangle the mysterious regions of the guitar fretboard and unlock your potential. *Fretboard Mastery* familiarizes you with all the shapes you need to know by applying them in real musical examples, thereby reinforcing and reaffirming your newfound knowledge. The result is a much higher level of comprehension and retention.
00695331 Book/CD Pack.........................$19.95

### FRETBOARD ROADMAPS – 2ND EDITION
ESSENTIAL GUITAR PATTERNS THAT ALL THE PROS KNOW AND USE
*by Fred Sokolow*
The updated edition of this bestseller features more songs, updated lessons, and a full audio CD! Learn to play lead and rhythm anywhere on the fretboard, in any key; play a variety of lead guitar styles; play chords and progressions anywhere on the fretboard; expand your chord vocabulary; and learn to think musically – the way the pros do.
00695941 Book/CD Pack.........................$14.95

### GUITAR AEROBICS
A 52-WEEK, ONE-LICK-PER-DAY WORKOUT PROGRAM FOR DEVELOPING, IMPROVING & MAINTAINING GUITAR TECHNIQUE
*by Troy Nelson*
From the former editor of *Guitar One* magazine, here is a daily dose of vitamins to keep your chops fine tuned! Musical styles include rock, blues, jazz, metal, country, and funk. Techniques taught include alternate picking, arpeggios, sweep picking, string skipping, legato, string bending, and rhythm guitar. These exercises will increase speed, and improve dexterity and pick- and fret-hand accuracy. The accompanying CD includes all 365 workout licks plus play-along grooves in every style at eight different metronome settings.
00695946 Book/CD Pack.........................$19.95

### GUITAR CLUES
OPERATION PENTATONIC
*by Greg Koch*
Join renowned guitar master Greg Koch as he clues you in to a wide variety of fun and valuable pentatonic scale applications. Whether you're new to improvising or have been doing it for a while, this book/CD pack will provide loads of delicious licks and tricks that you can use right away, from volume swells and chicken pickin' to intervallic and chordal ideas. The CD includes 65 demo and play-along tracks.
00695827 Book/CD Pack.........................$19.95

### INTRODUCTION TO GUITAR TONE & EFFECTS
*by David M. Brewster*
This book/CD pack teaches the basics of guitar tones and effects, with audio examples on CD. Readers will learn about: overdrive, distortion and fuzz • using equalizers • modulation effects • reverb and delay • multi-effect processors • and more.
00695766 Book/CD Pack.........................$14.95

### PICTURE CHORD ENCYCLOPEDIA
This comprehensive guitar chord resource for all playing styles and levels features five voicings of 44 chord qualities for all twelve keys – 2,640 chords in all! For each, there is a clearly illustrated chord frame, as well as *an actual photo* of the chord being played! Includes info on basic fingering principles, open chords and barre chords, partial chords and broken-set forms, and more.
00695224 .........................$19.95

### SCALE CHORD RELATIONSHIPS
*by Michael Mueller & Jeff Schroedl*
This book teaches players how to determine which scales to play with which chords, so guitarists will never have to fear chord changes again! This book/CD pack explains how to: recognize keys • analyze chord progressions • use the modes • play over nondiatonic harmony • use harmonic and melodic minor scales • use symmetrical scales such as chromatic, whole-tone and diminished scales • incorporate exotic scales such as Hungarian major and Gypsy minor • and much more!
00695563 Book/CD Pack.........................$14.95

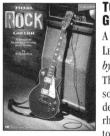

### SPEED MECHANICS FOR LEAD GUITAR
Take your playing to the stratosphere with the most advanced lead book by this proven heavy metal author. *Speed Mechanics* is the ultimate technique book for developing the kind of speed and precision in today's explosive playing styles. Learn the fastest ways to achieve speed and control, secrets to make your practice time really count, and how to open your ears and make your musical ideas more solid and tangible. Packed with over 200 vicious exercises including Troy's scorching version of "Flight of the Bumblebee." Music and examples demonstrated on CD. 89-minute audio.
00699323 Book/CD Pack.........................$19.95

### TOTAL ROCK GUITAR
A COMPLETE GUIDE TO LEARNING ROCK GUITAR
*by Troy Stetina*
This unique and comprehensive source for learning rock guitar is designed to develop both lead and rhythm playing. It covers: getting a tone that rocks • open chords, power chords and barre chords • riffs, scales and licks • string bending, strumming, palm muting, harmonics and alternate picking • all rock styles • and much more. The examples are in standard notation with chord grids and tab, and the CD includes full-band backing for all 22 songs.
00695246 Book/CD Pack.........................$19.99

---